COVER TO cover

BIBL
7 SE
AND

G000138520

Fruit of the *Spirit*

GROWING MORE LIKE JESUS

CWR

Selwyn Hughes
with Ian Sewter

Contents

Introduction

The fruit of the Spirit has been described as the nine qualities that go to make up Christian character. *The Message* paraphrases Paul's words in Galatians 5:22–23 beautifully:

> [God] brings gifts into our lives, much the same way that fruit appears in an orchard – things like affection for others, exuberance about life, serenity. We develop a willingness to stick with things, a sense of compassion in the heart, and a conviction that a basic holiness permeates things and people. We find ourselves involved in loyal commitments, not needing to force our way in life, able to marshal and direct our energies wisely.

The well-known Christian author John Stott says that Galatians 5:22–23 are his favourite verses in the Bible and that he meditates on these verses more than any others. May I suggest, as a helpful spiritual exercise over the next seven weeks, that you repeat these verses to yourself every day? You may be surprised at what happens.

It is important to note that when Paul speaks about the things that come from our sinful nature in Galatians 5:19–21 he calls them 'acts', but when talking about the qualities that come from the Spirit he calls them 'fruit'. 'Acts' points to something manufactured whereas 'fruit' suggests something that grows without effort – the result of the Spirit abiding within. The Church would be transformed in terms of relationships if every Christian manifested the nine qualities listed in this passage. We would not need to pray for revival because the wonderful signs of revival would already be apparent. People would come knocking at our door wanting to learn how to live.

Imparting the qualities listed in Galatians 5:22–23 is just one aspect of the Spirit's work in the life of a

Christian. Though this may be regarded by some as an oversimplification, it may be said that the Holy Spirit seeks to minister to us in two particular ways: to make us more pure and to impart to us spiritual power. Power is demonstrated through the gifts of the Spirit and purity through the fruit that we have set out to explore in this study. The two, I would say, are of equal importance. Many Christians claim that they are far more interested in the fruit of the Spirit than the gifts, but that is not what God wants. He wants us to be people who demonstrate both power and purity. So please be assured that in emphasising the fruit of the Spirit I am not intending to divert attention from the gifts of the Spirit and their miraculous nature or to put one before the other.

The indwelling of the Holy Spirit results in many things, and one of the most important is a quality of being which has nine characteristics. A number of Bible translations, including the Moffatt version, use the term 'harvest of the Spirit' rather than 'fruit of the Spirit', pointing to the finished product, the outcome. When we allow the Holy Spirit to take root in our hearts then the fruit produced is nine special qualities. Once the Holy Spirit resides within us we do not just become the recipients of pleasurable emotions, though of course that does happen. The divine indwelling makes us better persons. We must never forget that God's primary concern is to make us holy. But the holier we are the happier we will be. The Christian in whom the fruit of the Spirit is fully evident gives the best portrayal of saintliness it is possible to find.

How, then, does God go about painting a portrait of a saint? His canvas is the heart of one who is redeemed. The colours He puts on His palette are love, joy, peace, patience, kindness, goodness, faithfulness, humility and self-control. The absence of any one of these virtues would be serious, for every one is needed if the portrait is to be a masterpiece. And these colours are not pastel shades – each one is deep and rich and vibrant. The model He uses is the peerless example of His own dear Son, in whom every quality is seen to perfection and wonderfully balanced by every other. Even now, as you read these lines, His brush is at work, gently and lovingly caressing into your nature all the lineaments of your Lord's character. All He asks is that you hold still – that you stop trying and start trusting. Do this and, in the truest sense of the word, you will become a saint and bear fruit that will last and glorify Him.

This is God's great goal for your life – to mould you into the image of His dear Son. I like the way the Living Bible paraphrases Romans 8:29, 'For from the very beginning God decided that those who came to him... should become like his Son'. Isn't that beautiful? And the Holy Spirit has come within you in order to contribute to that great goal. How does He achieve such a tremendous task? By dispersing in our personalities the ingredients of Christ's nature, which Paul describes as the fruit of the Spirit. That is not to say we adopt an attitude of passivity in this process, but we actively seek the Holy Spirit's wisdom and help in the various situations we encounter in our lives. Using and applying the truths in this study guide can be an important step to becoming a more fruitful and Christlike disciple.

WEEK 1

The Primacy of Love

Opening Icebreaker

Cut up different fruits into small pieces and ask
blindfolded volunteers to taste and try to identify them.
It will be more interesting if you use some more unusual
fruits, such as passion fruit, kiwi and tomato. Then all
write a list of as many fruits as you can in a minute. What
are people's favourites and why?

Bible Readings

- Galatians 5:22–23
- John 15:1–17
- 1 Corinthians 13:1–13

Opening Our Eyes

The first fruit of the Spirit is 'love'. Love is the chief distinguishing mark of a child of God. Some regard the chief mark of a Christian as faith. But 1 Corinthians 13 says that even if we have faith that can move mountains but do not have love then we are nothing. Others say that truth is the greatest distinguishing mark of a Christian, but Paul tells us that even if we can fathom all mysteries and understand the truth about everything yet do not have love then again we are nothing.

Paul's mention in Galatians 5:22 of love as the first fruit of the Spirit fits in with his teaching in 1 Corinthians 13. Love, he claims, is greater than everything else – power, faith, service, and so on. If we examine 1 Corinthians 13 carefully we will see that every fruit of the Spirit mentioned in Galatians 5 is linked somewhere with this quality of supernatural love; either directly or by the use of synonyms, each of them is mentioned. Every other fruit proceeds from this first fruit of love. Notice the connection: love is patient – patience; love is kind – kindness; love does not envy – goodness; love does not boast and is not proud – gentleness; love is not self-seeking and is not easily angered – self-control and peace; love rejoices with the truth – joy; love always protects, always hopes, always perseveres – faithfulness.

Without love we are nothing. Indeed, I would go further and say that not only is love the first outcome of the Spirit within but that if love is lacking then everything is lacking. If you have the Spirit you will have love; if you do not have love you do not have the Spirit. It's as simple and as stark as that. The very first indication that we are growing spiritually is that we are growing in love and if we are growing in love then we are growing – period. If we are not growing in love then we are not growing in God, for His essential nature is love.

Ephesians 4:15, in the Moffatt translation, tells us that we are to 'hold by the truth, and by our love to grow up wholly into Him'. There is only one way to grow up 'wholly into Him' and that is 'by our love'. No matter how many good works we do, or how much of the Bible we know or have memorised, we will remain spiritually immature if we are not developing in love. Some think that if they start to love themselves more then they are fulfilling the scriptural commands to love, but if the love is ingrown and focused on the self then God's design for the personality is being violated. We are to love as we are loved. If the love is selectively applied to certain groups then again we are disobeying Jesus' command to love (John 13:34–35). We are mature to the extent that we can love and give out love to everybody. Indeed, any growth without growth in love is what has been described as 'sucker love' – growth that bears no fruit.

J.B. Phillips' translation of 1 Corinthians 8:1 explains the matter in this way: 'while knowledge may make a man look big, it is only love that can make him grow to his full stature.' Knowledge of the Bible is not enough. Love must also accompany it.

Discussion Starters

1. What are the keys to spiritual fruitfulness?

2. How is love related to other fruit of the Holy Spirit?

3. Why is love so important?

4. Do you agree that the word 'love' is devalued in modern society?

5. What two different types of love are revealed in Matthew 5:43–48?

6. Why are knowledge, faith, enthusiasm and hard work in church life insufficient? (See Rev. 2:1–7.)

_____

_____

_____

7. How can we grow in love?

_____

_____

_____

8. To what extent is love a choice or a feeling?

_____

_____

_____

9. Contrast God's love with human love.

_____

_____

_____

_____

10. How might God prune us so that we become more fruitful?

_____

_____

_____

_____

Personal Application

The nine qualities which are the fruit of the Spirit were all exemplified in Jesus' life on earth, and it is the present purpose of the Holy Spirit to graft them into us as we abide in Christ and maintain a close, day-by-day relationship with Him. When we allow the Spirit to work in our lives then the very first evidence of His presence is *agape* love. This is not a give-and-take kind of love, a love that is reciprocal; it is a love that descends from above and is showered on the deserving and the undeserving, the agreeable and the disagreeable. Christians who dwell deeply in God find that they are changed from people who just love occasionally, when it is convenient, to people whose controlling purpose is love. Love becomes the compelling motive and force in their lives.

Never, never try to manufacture love or create it in your heart. We love because we are loved, says the apostle John. Love originates not with us but with God. Linger in the shadow of the cross, for it is there that the love of God finds its most burning expression. When we perceive how much God loves us an amazing change is brought about in our personalities and we begin to love like Him. When we survey the wondrous cross, the place where the love of God was expressed most fully, the scales fall from our eyes and our own love flames in response.

Seeing Jesus in the Scriptures

'Greater love has no-one than this, that he lay down his life for his friends' (John 15:13).

WEEK 2

The Joy of Jesus

Opening Icebreaker

Recall a time when you have been 'full of joy', or briefly share the circumstances of an embarrassing or amusing incident.

Bible Readings

- Psalm 16:7–11
- Isaiah 12:1–6; 51:11
- Jeremiah 15:16
- Habakkuk 3:17–19
- Acts 16:16–34

Opening Our Eyes

We move on to consider the second fruit of the Spirit –
joy. It is not by accident that joy follows love because
joy is a by-product of love. If you concentrate on being
a joyful person joy will elude you. But if you concentrate
on being a loving person then joy will seek you out –
you will automatically be joyful. Sadly, many Christians
find it difficult to accept that joy is a fruit of the Spirit.
And not only do they not expect joy – they don't want
it either. They are under the lash of duty rather than the
canopy of delight. A grim Christian once told me, 'At
the heart of our faith is a cross. This means we ought
to be spending our time weeping, not laughing.' Well,
it is true that the cross is central to the Christian faith
and following Christ involves rigorous self-denial and
sometimes weeping, but this must be set against the fact
that the second fruit of the Spirit is joy. No one can deny
that from time to time each of us has to face suffering.
However, a Christian possesses a subterranean spring of
joy that will, if we allow it, burst upwards even in times
of suffering.

If there is no joy in our lives then we ought to question
if we really are allowing the Spirit to work in our hearts.
Joy, like love, is the essence of our faith. The empty tomb
takes away our empty gloom. We have an Easter morning
to celebrate in our faith, and that means there is always a
reason to rejoice.

When one woman experienced Christian conversion
she commented, 'It's strange, but I never associated joy
with God before.' How sad that so many think joy is
something reserved for the hereafter and do not expect
their faith to make them joyful now. Yet Jesus, in John
16:20–24, pointed out to the disciples that joy is part of
our present experience even here in this sin-soiled world.
Indeed in John 15:11 and 17:13, Jesus explained that He

had an inner joy and it was His joy that would fill His disciples. His joy and our joy are not different joys but one and the same. He says, 'My joy may be in you and... your joy may be complete.' His joy and our joy are not alien but allied. We are made in the inner structure of our beings for the joy of Jesus – His joy completes ours.

We can better understand this supernatural joy if we distinguish it from the pleasures of life with which it is sometimes confused. Spiritual joy is quite different from pleasure or happiness. A non-Christian can experience pleasure and happiness but he or she cannot experience supernatural joy. Indeed, worldly people often pride themselves on knowing how to experience pleasure. Yet happiness and Christian joy are definitely different. Happiness depends on what happens. It requires conditions to be favourable and thus it can be stolen from us by things like lack of money or even a toothache. Christian joy, however, is completely independent of circumstances. It is there in the believer even when strength and health and friends are gone – when circumstances are not only unkind but savage. Out of all the miracles I have witnessed in my life, none is more wonderful than seeing Christ's exuberant joy burst forth in those who are caught up in pain or persecution. That joy can prove triumphant is not just a theory but a glorious fact.

Discussion Starters

1. Why does a Christian always have a reason to rejoice?

_____

_____

_____

2. What is the difference between happiness and true joy?

_____

_____

_____

3. Why do some people imagine God as grim-faced rather than full of joy?

_____

_____

_____

_____

4. How can we experience the joy of Jesus?

_____

_____

_____

5. Why may joy elude us?

_____

_____

_____

6. Why is joy an important fruit of the Holy Spirit?

7. What do you think God enjoys?

8. How can 'the joy of the LORD' make us strong?

9. What are the inward and outward expressions of joy?

10. How are salvation and God's Word linked with joy?

Personal Application

An important aspect of joy is that it protects our hearts against problem emotions. Jealousy or anxiety can quickly find a lodging place in a heart that has no joy. But as the heart is filled with joy the problem emotions are forced out. Joy also keeps us alert and alive spiritually. Disease germs, we are told, cause most harm to a body debilitated by despondency, because the immune system has been weakened. The same thing happens in the realm of the soul. Harmful thoughts and emotions invade the soul with ease when there is no joy, and start to destroy the health of the soul. Joy, however, gives them no room. It immunises the spirit against attack.

So joy is not just the bloom of health; it is the soul's protection also, for the 'joy of the LORD is your strength' (Neh. 8:10). Every Christian should be conscious of joy flowing through the soul as a consequence of receiving Christ, so if it is not flowing, something must be blocking it. Clear away the obstacles and joy flows automatically. If you are conscious that you lack this deep abiding joy then look within. What are the hindrances? Consider them and remove them and then joy will flow. God is not withholding Himself, and you must not withhold yourself. When you meet God, joy is inevitable.

Seeing Jesus in the Scriptures

'Let us fix our eyes on Jesus, the author and perfecter of our faith, who for the joy set before him endured the cross, scorning its shame, and sat down at the right hand of the throne of God' (Heb. 12:2).

WEEK 3

The Peace of God

Opening Icebreaker

Read aloud together, 'Aim for perfection, listen to my appeal, be of one mind, live in peace. And the God of love and peace will be with you... May the grace of the Lord Jesus Christ, and the love of God, and the fellowship of the Holy Spirit be with you all'. Exchange the sign of peace with one another.

Bible Readings

- Psalm 119:165
- Matthew 6:25–34
- Romans 5:1–2; 8:5–9
- Philippians 4:4–9
- 2 Thessalonians 3:16

Opening Our Eyes

We move on now to the third fruit of the Spirit – peace. The order is an inspired one: first love because love is pre-eminent, then joy because joy comes as a result of love, and then peace which is the consequence of joy. This sequence is significant. When we love with the love that Jesus puts in our heart by His Spirit then joy and peace follow as natural consequences. 'Peace,' said someone, 'is joy grown quiet and assured.' A preacher once compared joy and peace in this way: 'Joy is peace with its hat thrown high in the air and peace is joy with its arms folded in serene assurance.'

Once again it is important to remember that peace is not something that can be manufactured. We cannot create it any more than we can create any of the other fruit of the Spirit. It is divinely given – a glorious consequence of God's presence in the soul. Jesus knew this kind of peace and He offers the same serenity to every one of His disciples: 'my peace I give you... Do not let your hearts be troubled' (John 14:27). When we remain in Christ we are given a peace that not only transcends all understanding – but all misunderstanding also.

Peace is not passivity. Some people are abnormally inactive and unreactive by temperament. By nature they just seem to let the world wash by and take no resolute attitude to life at all. It is possible to look at someone with a temperament like this and conclude that they are manifesting the fruit of the Spirit. But passivity is as far removed from peace as chalk is from cheese. One is natural, the other supernatural. Peace is not achieved by mental gymnastics. Today's world is full of 'mind-healers' who promise that if you attend their seminars or enrol on their courses they will give you the poise and self-assurance you always wanted. An advertisement I come across frequently in the newspapers says, 'Let us show you how to achieve peace of mind.' The phrase 'peace of mind' in itself reveals the shallowness of the approach. You cannot have genuine peace of mind until you have peace in the depths of your spirit. It is impossible to have peace of mind if there is conflict in your spirit. The peace which is the fruit of the Spirit brings peace to the mind because the mind is under the control of that part of our being which the Bible calls the 'spirit' – the motivating centre of our lives. When peace flows there, then, and only then, can a person experience true peace of mind.

Although peace is something given rather than something achieved, its continuance is guaranteed only as we fulfil certain conditions. If, for example, we decide to go on an immoral spree, we will soon find that peace eludes us. Scripture tells us, 'There is no peace... for the wicked' (Isa. 57:21). Why? Because peace is conditional on obedience to God's moral code. Isaiah 26:3 says, 'You will keep him in perfect peace, whose mind is stayed on You' (NKJV). Notice the words 'stayed on You'. This shows that in order to enjoy continuous peace there must be a conscious centring on God. He must not be the place of occasional reference but of continuous reference. Furthermore, He must be the centre of our trust, for it is only as we trust Him, that our hearts and minds are guarded from anxiety.

Discussion Starters

1. How can we experience the peace of God?

_____

_____

_____

_____

2. How can we continue to experience the peace of God?

_____

_____

_____

_____

3. What situations may cause you to be troubled?

_____

_____

_____

_____

4. How is faith linked to peace?

_____

_____

_____

_____

5. Why is passivity or stillness not the same as the peace of God?

_____

_____

_____

_____

6. How do you consciously centre on God?

_____

_____

_____

_____

7. Is it difficult to believe that nothing can happen to us without God's permission?

_____

_____

_____

_____

8. How can the peace of God guard our hearts and minds?

_____

_____

_____

_____

9. Why may Christians have peace with God but not experience the peace of God?

_____

_____

_____

_____

10. How is experiencing the peace of God linked to prayer?

_____

_____

_____

_____

Personal Application

A Christian who truly believes in God – who does not pretend to believe, or only half-believes – will inevitably experience God's perfect peace. Job 22:21 says, 'Quit quarrelling with God! Agree with him and you will have peace at last!' (Living Bible). But what does it mean to believe in God? A Christian believes – and believes wholeheartedly – that Jesus is God and that He is the Saviour of the world (see Rom. 10:9; Titus 2:13). A Christian also believes that the universe is in the keeping of Infinite Wisdom and Infinite Love, and that God is directing the course of our life (see Psa. 139:16). Nothing can happen in the universe without God's permission. The peace of a Christian is therefore established on the rock of reality – the foundation for perfect peace.

Seeing Jesus in the Scriptures

The disciples were in a boat on the Sea of Galilee when a fierce storm descended causing them to become exceedingly frightened. There were thirteen storms in the boat that night – one on the lake and twelve in the hearts of the disciples. But where was Jesus? Asleep in the stern of the boat. Our Lord enjoyed the best possible peace – sleep – in the worst possible place – the stern of the boat in a storm. We see another demonstration of this deep serenity our Lord enjoyed when, as the ugly arms of the cross stretched out to take Him, He said, 'Peace I leave with you; my peace I give you' (John 14:27). In the words of W.E. Sangster, 'Galilee in storm and Calvary in darkness both set it off.'

WEEK 4

Patient with Everyone

Opening Icebreaker

Describe situations which cause you to become frustrated.
What is the longest you have ever had to wait for
something and how did you feel? How have others been
affected by your lack of patience?

Bible Readings

- Ecclesiastes 7:8–9
- Mark 3:1–6
- Ephesians 4:20–27
- 1 Thessalonians 5:12–18
- James 1:19–21

Opening Our Eyes

The central meaning of this word 'patience' is 'good temper'. It denotes a person who does not easily 'fly off the handle'. He or she maintains good temper amid the inevitable ups and downs of life events.

Did Jesus ever lose His temper? There are those who think He did and would point to the cleansing of the Temple or particularly the way He responded to the Pharisees. I once heard a Christian defend his inability to remain good tempered in all situations in this way: 'If Jesus could not control His temper when faced with the scorn of the Pharisees in Mark 3, and tore them off a strip, then why should I be criticised for my inability to control mine?' But did the behaviour of Jesus on this occasion result from a loss of temper? I do not believe so. One luminous phrase lights up the story and puts the matter, I feel, in its proper perspective: 'deeply distressed at their stubborn hearts'. Do you see it? The reason why Jesus 'looked round at them in anger' was because He was 'deeply distressed at their stubborn hearts'. The cause of His anger was distress, not loss of temper – distress caused by their insensibility to human need. It was distress caused by what was happening to someone else, not personal pique at what was happening to Him.

When we get angry it is usually because our ego has been wounded and hits back, not in redemption, but in retaliation. There is a temper that is redemptive and there is a temper that is retaliatory. The redemptive temper burns with the steady fire of redemptive intention; the retaliatory temper simply burns you up. It is intended to burn the other person up, but all it serves to do is to burn you. Patience that is the fruit of the Spirit works in us – if we let it – to temper our purposes to kingdom purposes, and to kingdom purposes alone.

Although Jesus was free from bad temper, He was not free from tension. I am using the word 'tension' in the sense of being in a state of moderate stress. It's interesting that the translator James Moffatt renders Luke 12:50 in this way: 'I have a baptism to undergo – what tension I suffer, till it is all over!' A certain amount of tension is a necessary part of life. Jesus experienced it, and so will we. It is not always a bad thing. The violin string that is free from tension is incapable of producing music, but when tightened it gives forth a sound that delights the ear. The tension that Jesus felt was a tension that was harnessed to the interests of others. He was on His way to a cross, and the tension would not end until He pronounced the words, 'It is finished' (John 19:30).

This tension, however, did not leave Jesus frustrated and bad tempered; it left Him calm and composed, with a prayer for the forgiveness of His enemies upon His lips. It drove Him, not to pieces, but to peace – the peace of achievement and victory. This was because the tension was harnessed to God's perfect will – hence it was a constructive urge. Unfortunately, many of our tensions drive us, not towards pursuing God's will, but towards pursuing our own will. We are more concerned for ourselves than for the divine interests. This kind of driving will succeed only in driving us to distraction.

Discussion Starters

1. Why is our temper a good measure of our patience?

_____

_____

_____

_____

2. Why may things that make us tense and angry not be an example of a bad temper?

_____

_____

_____

_____

3. Why is a certain amount of tension a necessary, inevitable and useful part of life?

_____

_____

_____

_____

4. What makes people lose their temper and how do they find it again?

_____

_____

_____

_____

5. What are the key differences between a temper that is based on redemption and a temper based on retaliation?

_____

_____

_____

_____

6. How did Jesus handle tense situations?

_____

_____

_____

_____

7. What do you think lies behind incidents of 'road rage', 'computer rage' etc?

_____

_____

_____

8. Why should we not let the sun go down while we are still angry?

_____

_____

_____

9. How do you handle tense situations in such a way that you avoid becoming angry?

_____

_____

_____

Personal Application

For it is commendable if a man bears up under the pain of unjust suffering because he is conscious of God. But how is it to your credit if you receive a beating for doing wrong and endure it? But if you suffer for doing good and you endure it, this is commendable before God. To this you were called, because Christ suffered for you, leaving you an example that you should follow in his steps.

'He committed no sin,
and no deceit was found in his mouth.'

When they hurled their insults at him, he did not retaliate; when he suffered, he made no threats. Instead, he entrusted himself to him who judges justly. He himself bore our sins in his body on the tree, so that we might die to sins and live for righteousness; by his wounds you have been healed. For you were like sheep going astray, but now you have returned to the Shepherd and Overseer of your souls. (1 Pet. 2:19–25)

'Better a patient man than a warrior, a man who controls his temper than one who takes a city' (Prov. 16:32). The next time you feel you are losing your temper ask the Holy Spirit for the fruit of patience.

Seeing Jesus in the Scriptures

'When they came to the place called the Skull, there they crucified him, along with the criminals – one on his right, the other on his left. Jesus said, "Father, forgive them, for they do not know what they are doing"' (Luke 23:33–34).

Despite the most extreme provocation and injustice, Jesus kept His temper and responded in love, forgiveness and mercy.

WEEK 5

Supernatural Kindness and Goodness

Opening Icebreaker

Can you recall an incident when someone was especially kind to you, and how that made you feel?

Bible Readings

- Romans 15:14
- Galatians 2:20
- Philippians 2:14–16
- Colossians 3:1–17

Opening Our Eyes

The fifth fruit of the Spirit listed in Galatians 5:22 is kindness. 'Kindness' is a very beautiful word; it means 'a kindly disposition, or warm goodwill towards others'. In recent times Mother Teresa gave this instruction: 'Be the living expression of God's kindness... give... not only your care, but also your heart.' It is not a false sentimentality or foolish indulgence but a supernatural virtue endowed by the Holy Spirit which pervades our whole disposition and engenders within us a warm goodwill to others. To speak, for example, of an 'unkind Christian' is almost a contradiction in terms. There is some evidence that in the early centuries of the Church, non-Christians used the words 'kindly' and 'Christian' as synonyms. Tertullian, one of the Church Fathers, said, 'The words were so allied in meaning that no harm was done by the confusion.'

Kindness is not being a 'do-gooder'. Many think, for example, that kindness is demonstrated by giving money to people who have a financial need. But giving money to people who appear to need it without being guided by the Spirit can result in great harm. The supernatural kindness that is a gift of the Spirit can sometimes appear to be severe because it is motivated by love and therefore knows when to give a hard refusal. It is based on God's kindness, which can cut with the same firmness that a surgeon uses when he is intent on removing a life-threatening tumour. We must never forget that it is kindness in the heart of God that leads Him to rid us of those moral tumours that threaten our spiritual health. But always God's severity is our security. It is redemptive and for our best.

Most commentators agree that 'goodness' is the hardest fruit to define, as the word 'good' is used so widely that it can mean almost everything and nearly nothing. It is the view of most writers and Bible commentators that supernatural goodness is not just a matter of doing good things (though it includes that) but that it is essential goodness – goodness in the inner parts. Edwin Chaplin, a Christian writer, put it well when he said, 'Goodness consists not just in the outward things we do but in the inward thing we are.' Goodness, like kindness, has first to be an attitude before it becomes an action. In fact, some commentators are of the opinion that it is more non-verbal than verbal – it is evidenced not so much in words as in one's whole demeanour. And that demeanour is the character of Christ flowing in and through one of His followers. Perhaps we can get no nearer to a definition of supernatural goodness than this: reminding people of Jesus Christ.

George Müller of Bristol, the man who cared for so many orphans in the nineteenth century, was said to demonstrate the fruit of goodness to a remarkable degree. He was once asked what he considered to be the power behind his ministry. He surprised his questioner by talking about his 'secret death'. He said, 'I died to George Müller, his opinions, preferences, tastes and will; died to the world, its approval or censure; died to the approval or blame even of my brethren and friends; and since then I have studied only to show myself approved of God.' In those who manifest the fruit of goodness, one thing is always clear: they have died to their own interests and have returned to live for the interests of Christ.

Discussion Starters

1. What is your own definition of kindness?

_____
_____
_____
_____

2. What is your own definition of goodness?

_____
_____
_____
_____

3. How do goodness and kindness differ?

_____
_____
_____
_____

4. Why is kindness a defining quality of a Christian?

_____
_____
_____
_____

5. What key elements of spiritual fruit are revealed in the quote of Mother Teresa?

_____
_____
_____
_____

6. Do you agree with the proverb that: 'sometimes we need to be cruel to be kind'?

7. How can antonyms of the word goodness reveal more of its own qualities?

8. How can synonyms of the word goodness help us understand it better?

9. What do you understand by the term 'secret death' when applied to Christians?

10. Why may self-interest prevent goodness developing in our lives?

Personal Application

Because kindness can minister such comfort and encouragement, how imperative it is that we ask God to ripen this fruit within us. Of the many things associated with Paul's shipwreck on Malta, Luke recalls in particular that the 'islanders showed us unusual kindness' (Acts 28:2). Kindness is often manifested in acts of benevolence done out of a desire to please the Lord Jesus Christ. In Matthew 25:31–46 we see that as we minister to others through acts of kindness we are actually ministering to Christ Himself.

Christians in whom 'goodness' is growing will not 'use' others but will love them for themselves alone. They will not mentally fit people into their schemes for they have no schemes. Although it is true that the essence of goodness is to be found to some degree in all Christians, in those who have known what it is to die to self it overflows. Such believers exude goodness. So, in yearning for this fruit of the Spirit to be produced more abundantly in your life, let us keep in mind that it manifests itself not when we strain to be good but when we surrender to goodness. The more we abide in Christ and base our lives on His teaching the more kindness and goodness will grow in us.

Seeing Jesus in the Scriptures

Although Jesus was a peasant carpenter from despised Nazareth, He exuded goodness. We also see on many occasions His kindness when He had compassion on the sick (Matt. 14:14; Mark 1:41), the hungry (Matt. 15:32), the lost (Mark 6:34), and the bereaved (Luke 7:11–15).

WEEK 6

Reliable Faithfulness

Opening Icebreaker

Place these people in the order you would trust them and explain your reasons: parent, politician, policeman, publican, prostitute, professor, painter, priest, passer-by, pawnbroker, plumber, publicist, preacher.

Bible Readings

- Luke 8:4–15; 16:10–15
- Acts 5:1–11

Opening Our Eyes

Now we start to examine the seventh fruit of the Spirit
– faithfulness. Faithfulness is the quality of reliability or
trustworthiness which not only relates to God but makes
a Christian someone on whom others can utterly rely
and whose word they can utterly accept. We must not
think that because faithfulness is listed among the last
three qualities on Paul's list it is of lesser importance.
So important is it that Jesus says, 'Whoever is faithful'
(Moffatt) 'with very little can also be trusted with much,
and whoever is dishonest with very little will also be
dishonest with much' (Luke 16:10). Nobody gets away
with anything dishonest in a moral universe. Something
dies in us the moment we are dishonest – not least our
self-respect. Death eats away at our hearts the moment
dishonesty is let in. We are not so much punished *for* our
sin as *by* our sin.

In my opinion faithfulness is often sadly lacking in
God's children. There are professing Christians who
seem to think that matters such as tax evasion or making
telephone calls from their office without permission do
not have a direct bearing on their Christian life. Look
again at what Jesus said in Luke 16:11 in the Moffatt
translation: 'If you are not faithful with dishonest
mammon, how can you ever be trusted with true Riches?'
Here the basic principles are laid down. If you are not
faithful with the trifling, you will not be faithful with
the tremendous. If you are not faithful with the material
(mammon), how can you expect to be entrusted with
the spiritual – 'true Riches'? Notice how Moffatt spells
the word 'riches' with a capital 'R'. Why is this? Because
spiritual richness is so great that you just have to spell it
with a capital 'R'. But Jesus says one more thing: 'if you
are not faithful with what belongs to another, how can
you ever be given what is your own?' (v12, Moffatt). It's
a sad fact, but nevertheless true, that often those who are

not faithful with other people's possessions finish up with
nothing of their own.

There are four main characteristics of the fruit of the Spirit
which Paul terms 'faithfulness' – honesty, reliability, a
deep concern for truth and a willingness to carry through
on all God's commands to us – keeping faith to the end.
Luke 8:15 in the Moffatt translation reads, 'As for the seed
in the good soil, that means those who hear and hold
fast the word in a good, sound heart, and so bear fruit
steadfastly.' Notice the words 'so bear fruit steadfastly';
they teach us that only the steadfast are finally fruitful.
It is those who persevere and remain faithful through
opposition, sickness, disappointment, temptation and so
on that will produce a hundredfold.

D.L. Moody, the great American preacher who lived in
the nineteenth century, said: 'If we could get people who
put their hand to the plough to decide that they will
never draw back no matter what the wind or weather,
what a powerful Church we would have.' Powerful
indeed. It's so sad that because we fail, the Church is not
what it could be. How many of us, I wonder, are guilty
of breaking promises and only half fulfilling tasks? Whose
fault is it? It cannot be the fault of the Holy Spirit, for He
dwells in us to provide the power to see things through –
if we let Him.

Discussion Starters

1. What are the key characteristics of faithfulness and which is weakest in your own life?

2. Why is faithfulness much more than regularly attending church, praying and reading your Bible?

3. Why is faithfulness so important?

4. What keys to fruitfulness do we find in the parable of the sower?

5. How do our daily material lives at work, home or school affect our spiritual lives?

_____

_____

_____

_____

6. What challenges do you personally face in terms of faithfulness and reliability?

_____

_____

_____

_____

7. What effect do the media, TV and films have on standards of honesty and faithfulness?

_____

_____

_____

_____

8. How may the world, the flesh and the devil attack our determination to be faithful?

_____

_____

_____

_____

9. What did Ananias and Sapphira do wrong?

_____

_____

_____

_____

Personal Application

The minister of a large church was asked what was the outstanding need of his congregation. He said, 'Faithfulness. Fifty per cent of my church members are hangers-on who are getting a free ride and contributing nothing from purse or person. Twenty-five per cent promise to do something and then, after a few stabs at it, drop out. They lack fidelity. The life of this church is carried on by the remaining twenty-five per cent.' Let's aim to be one of the faithful.

Seeing Jesus in the Scriptures

'[Christ] had to be made like his brothers in every way, in order that he might become a merciful and faithful high priest in service to God, and that he might make atonement for the sins of the people. Because he himself suffered when he was tempted, he is able to help those who are being tempted.

Therefore, holy brothers, who share in the heavenly calling, fix your thoughts on Jesus, the apostle and high priest whom we confess. He was faithful to the one who appointed him, just as Moses was faithful in all God's house. Jesus has been found worthy of greater honour than Moses, just as the builder of a house has greater honour than the house itself. For every house is built by someone, but God is the builder of everything. Moses was faithful as a servant in all God's house, testifying to what would be said in the future. But Christ is faithful as a son over God's house. And we are his house, if we hold on to our courage and the hope of which we boast' (Heb. 2:17–3:6).

WEEK 7

Humility and Self-control

Opening Icebreaker

What made Jesus humble even though He was God the Son? Why was Moses described as 'more humble than anyone else on the face of the earth' (Num. 12:3) even though he led a nation and ordered judicial executions?

Bible Readings

- Proverbs 16:19–20; 23:1–5; 24:30–34
- Romans 12:1–8
- Philippians 2:1–11

Opening Our Eyes

The words 'humble' and 'gentle' are found together a number of times in the New Testament, as, for example, in Matthew 11:29, 'I am gentle and humble in heart' (also Eph. 4:2 and Col. 3:12). The Christian in whom the Spirit dwells is a person who is gentle and humble. It has been said that apart from love, nothing is more characteristic of a Christian, and nothing more caricatured and misunderstood than humility. The world has never had much time for gentleness or humility, confusing it with self-belittlement, lack of ambition, an inferiority complex or what the ancients described as a 'servile grovelling spirit'. To truly understand humility calls for a piercing spiritual perception which is given only to those who know God.

Phillips Brooks, a great American preacher, once said, 'The true way to be humble is not to stoop until you are smaller than yourself, but to stand at your real height against some higher nature that will show you what the real smallness of your greatness is. Stand at your highest, and then look at Christ, then go away and forever be humble.' The truly humble are conscious of greatness before they are conscious of humility.

The ninth and last fruit of the Spirit is self-control. Underlying the word is the idea of self-restraint, mastery of one's personality and a controlled and disciplined nature. When the Holy Spirit is at work in our lives He not only gives us the power to do what we should but also the power not to do what is wrong. Various philosophies over past centuries have all sought to produce a happy and contented person through self-control. Some have advocated thought-control, some breath-control, others will-control. The Christian way is different – it produces joyful and contented people, not primarily by thought-control or even will-control, but by Christ-control. Christians are people who are self-controlled, but we become that not by self-effort alone but through the gracious work of the Holy Spirit who lives within us. We do not gain the things of the Spirit through self-control; we gain self-control through the presence of the Spirit in our lives. It is not so much self-control as control of the self.

What are some of the areas of life in which we need to control the self? Let me select what I consider to be the three most important. The first is the area of sex. Within the boundaries of God's design, sex is wonderfully creative and satisfying, but when sex is unrestrained and without boundaries it becomes chaotic, often resulting in difficult and complicated consequences.

Another area in which we need self-control is that of the tongue. James points out that the tongue is an important indicator of how well we control ourselves (see James 3:2–12). There are three stages, we are told, in verbal communication: impulse, consideration and speech. Many omit the second and jump from impulse to speech. The person who has self-control pauses between impulse and speech and gives himself or herself to consideration.

The third area is that which has to do with bodily indulgence. The body, by its very nature, is comfort-loving, but too much comfort is debilitating. The body is not an enemy to be punished or destroyed but we do need to control our desires for things like food, luxuries and laziness.

Discussion Starters

1. What are examples of false humility?

_____

_____

_____

_____

2. What are examples of true spiritual humility?

_____

_____

_____

_____

3. Why is humility an important fruit of the Holy Spirit?

_____

_____

_____

_____

4. How would you describe the characteristics of a 'haughty' spirit?

_____

_____

_____

_____

5. How can we seek to develop the fruit of humility in our lives?

_____

_____

_____

_____

6. What are key areas where we need self-control?

_____

_____

_____

_____

7. In which areas of life do you personally need more self-control?

_____

_____

_____

_____

8. Why may a lack of self-control limit our spiritual maturity and fruitfulness?

_____

_____

_____

_____

9. Why is self-control more accurately described as control of the self?

_____

_____

_____

_____

10. What are your deepest impressions of our study on spiritual fruit?

_____

_____

_____

_____

The Fruit of the Spir

Personal Application

One of the first marks of true humility is a teachable spirit – an attitude that recognises our own ignorance and accepts the fact that without God's help we cannot understand the depths of truth. Those who approach the Bible with a proud and know-all attitude will find it firmly shut and it will not reveal anything to them. That is why we need to pray with the psalmist, 'Open my eyes that I may see wonderful things in your law' (Psa. 119:18). God declared through Isaiah, 'I dwell… With him who has a contrite and humble spirit' (Isa. 57:15, NKJV). James says, 'God opposes the proud' (James 4:6). Do you realise what that means? The great and omnipotent God actually repel the approaches of the proud. As Psalm 138:6 tells us, the proud He knows only from afar; it is to the humble that He gives grace. Reading and meditating on passages such as Job 38–41 and Isaiah 40 emphasise the greatness of God and our total reliance upon Him which helps produce in us a spirit of humility.

Are there areas of your life that are out of control? Present yourself to God anew as a living sacrifice and seek the help of the Holy Spirit for Christ to bring His control that you may be transformed into His likeness.

Seeing Jesus in the Scriptures

'During the days of Jesus' life on earth, he offered up prayers and petitions with loud cries and tears to the one who could save him from death, and he was heard because of his reverent submission' (Heb. 5:7).

Leader's Notes

Week 1: The Primacy of Love

Opening Icebreaker
There is no great theological truth to this icebreaker! It is merely designed to encourage people to think about fruit and how God has introduced amazing variety, beautiful colour and enjoyable tastes into His world.

Bible Readings
Although the subject of this week's study is love, as it is the first in the series, we also read the passage in John 15 which refers to fruit in more general terms and discover that God has specifically chosen us to bear fruit. This is not an optional extra but a vital part of our Christian lives.

Aim of the Session
The aim of the session is to introduce the subject of the fruit of the Holy Spirit and then focus on the primacy of love. It would be helpful to refer to the Introduction and specifically make the point that these qualities are not the result of human effort but rather of allowing God to plant, water, prune and nurture these supernatural characteristics within us. However, He does seek and require our co-operation. In the parable of the sower it was the quality of the soil that determined the fruitfulness of the seed. Weeds of anxiety, thorns of materialism, shallow roots of commitment and renunciation under persecution can choke the good seed that God sows in our hearts (Mark 4:1–20).

What exactly does Scripture mean when it uses the word 'love'? In English the word 'love' has a variety of meanings. It is used for the mighty passion that moves in the heart of God but it is used also in connection with such things as a love of chocolate, the flutterings of the adolescent heart in spring, or even an extramarital affair. The one word 'love' has to cover a multiplicity of diverse meanings. The Greek language is much richer in this respect. It has four words for love. *Eros* is love between the sexes. *Philia* means affectionate human (friendship) love. *Storge* is love within a family. The most powerful word for love, however, is *agape*, which means unconditional love – the love that surges in the heart of God. Everything God does is motivated by love. He can do nothing without love being the controlling factor. When Paul says in Galatians 5:22 that 'the fruit of the Spirit is love', the word he uses for 'love' is *agape*. The love we are expected to experience and demonstrate when we are indwelt by the Spirit is not a general kind of love but love of a specific kind – God's own sacrificial *agape* love.

Paul says in 2 Corinthians 5:14, 'For Christ's love compels us'. It is possible to be compelled by the love of achievement, of success, of a cause, of a fight. What compels us – the love of a cause or the love of Christ? The enemies of the early Christians complained that 'these followers of Jesus love each other even before they are acquainted'. They did. They couldn't help it, for the very nature of the faith they had embraced was love.

How though can love be demonstrated? Love is an attitude that translates into actions. For example, 'For God so loved the world that he gave his one and only Son' (John 3:16). It has been suggested that love can be expressed in five key ways. *Gifts* have always been an expression of showing love, but also spending *time* with people, *acts of service or helping*, using *words of appreciation or affection*, and *physical touch* (1 Pet. 5:14) are all means of demonstrating love. How good are group members at showing love? You could all score yourselves out of ten for each of the five ways to identify areas for growth.

Week 2: The Joy of Jesus

Opening Icebreaker

There are so many things that God has given us for which we can be joyful and thankful. It could be as simple as bird song, a beautiful garden or sunset, a newborn baby or a shared experience with friends. Recalling such memories will help prepare our minds and hearts for our study on joy.

Bible Readings

The readings highlight that God is a God of joy and that knowing Him and especially experiencing His salvation brings joy into our lives. Habakkuk emphasises that spiritual joy is independent of circumstance and this theme is reiterated by the story of Paul and Silas in Philippi. They were beaten 'black and blue' with 'rods that again and again slashed down across their bared backs' (Living Bible) and then clamped in leg irons in prison. Despite all this, they prayed and sang praises to God. In fact their joyful response to such a beating meant, 'the other prisoners could not believe their ears' (*The Message*).

Aim of the Session

We need to understand the source and nature of true spiritual joy if we are to experience the fullness of the Christian life. The Greek word *chara* translated 'joy' is a robust word. It is not resignation wearing a wan smile. The joy spoken of is exuberant and overflowing. The summons to rejoice is sounded no less than 70 times in the New Testament, and the word *chara* occurs close on 60 times. The New Testament really is a book of joy. Dr William Barclay claimed that joy is the distinctive atmosphere of the Christian life. 'Whatever the ingredients of Christian experience,' he said, 'and in whatever proportions they are mixed together, joy is one of them.' Even in the days after the death of my wife, I was wonderfully conscious of Christ's joy quietly breaking through the layers of my sadness and grief. Joy is always present in the heart of a Christian. It may not always be felt or recognised, but it is always there. And eventually it will break through to the surface, no matter what our situation or our circumstances. Present joy is often linked with future hope and what more joyous hope could a Christian possibly have for the future of experiencing eternal joy in God's presence?

It is vitally important to differentiate between spiritual joy and mere pleasure. Pleasures come and go. Look back over your life for a moment and think of the different things that have given you pleasure over the years. Perhaps, when you were a child, it was a bicycle, a football, or a doll. Then, when you entered your teens, it was something else. A relationship, perhaps, or a sport. In later years the things that gave you pleasure changed again. The theatre, books, an armchair ... the things that give us pleasure change over the years. But the joy of God is constant. Yet another difference between pleasure and joy is this: pleasure satiates. It is easy to have too much. And when the point of satiety is passed a sense of revulsion can set in. The things for which we once craved become repulsive to us. Joy, however, never satiates. A Christian says, 'We have enough, yet not too much to long for more.' Unlike pleasure, the joy that is the fruit of the Spirit remains with us constantly – even in times of difficulty, as Paul could testify (2 Cor. 6:10).

Scripture tells of various things that bring God special joy. For example, faith (Heb. 11:6), repentant sinners (Luke 15:7), praise (Heb. 13:15), giving (Heb. 13:16), unselfish prayer (1 Kings 3:7–13) and a righteous lifestyle (Prov. 16:7; 1 Thess. 4:1; 1 John 3:22).

Week 3: The Peace of God

Opening Icebreaker
A simple exercise to read Scripture aloud together and
then bless one another with the words, 'Peace be with
you'. This should help us realise and affirm that God's
peace is part of our heritage as Christians. The scripture
is from the end of 2 Corinthians 13.

Bible Readings
Guilt, anxiety and stress adversely affect the quality of
many people's lives. The Scriptures remind us that firstly,
because of Christ, we can have peace *with* God and then
through the Word of God and the Spirit of God we can
experience the peace *of* God.

Aim of the Session
The aim of the session is to show that the peace of God
is a tangible fruit of the Spirit and is available to every
believer. Peace is not the product of human temperament,
endeavour or even private hermit-like withdrawal. At
recurring intervals in the life of the Christian Church
various forms of withdrawal have been practised with a
view to discovering inner peace. Early Methodism was
almost wrecked by a form of it known as 'Stillness'.
The idea was to withdraw from all activity and discover
'stillness' before the Lord. This kind of stillness is not
to be confused with the supernatural peace which the
Spirit brings to the hearts of God's people. Stillness is
something achieved; peace is something given and that
God-given peace blossoms even in times of great activity.

William Barclay says that the word 'peace' came into
the New Testament with a great history. It corresponds
to the Hebrew word *shalom*. In classical Greek 'peace'
was mainly negative, implying freedom from war or
hostilities, but in the New Testament the word gathers up
the positive elements conveyed by the word *shalom*. The

central meaning is serenity and harmony. 'Peace' occurs 88 times in the New Testament, and it appears in every book except 1 John. This makes the New Testament a book of peace.

Peace is found in knowing and following God's will for our lives. Those who know the Spirit's perfect peace are those who do not simply resign themselves to God's will but rejoice in the realisation that His will is always best. This attitude is beautifully expressed by Mary who said, 'I am the Lord's servant ... May it be to me as you have said' (Luke 1:38). The devotional writer, Francis de Sales, summed it up in this way:

To rejoice in God's will suggests mobility – the mobility of a voyager who moves with the motion of the vessel on which he has embarked. It suggests also the abandonment of a servant in attendance on his lord, going only where his master goes. It is the attitude of a child leaving to his mother the care of willing, choosing and acting for him, content to be in her safe and tender keeping.

The biographer of Sadhu Sundar Singh, the great Indian Christian, says, 'Realise that to the Sadhu, as to Paul, partnership with Christ was a passion and a privilege that transformed hardship, labour and loss from something which was to be accepted negatively as an unfortunate necessity into something positively welcomed for His sake – and you will understand a little of the secret of the Sadhu's peace.' Our Lord, of course, is our supreme example in this. In the words of Robert Nicoll, 'He did not merely accept the will of God when it was brought to Him and laid upon Him. Rather, He went out to meet that loving will and fell upon its neck and kissed it.' Saints down the ages have illustrated through their lives the quality of this perfect peace; so can we!

Week 4: Patient with Everyone

Opening Icebreaker
The icebreaker should help people to realise the practical nature and personal application of this session.

Bible Reading
The readings reveal that patience is not just a nice quality but an essential characteristic of a godly life.

Aim of the Session
We need to understand how to handle tense situations without losing our temper. Remember that the word 'temper' simply means 'a disposition of mind' and really requires the words 'good' or 'bad' to define it. In the USA I once saw a sign on a car that read, 'Honk away – it's your ulcer.' Ulcers are usually physical symptoms of an ulcerated spirit – ulcerated by irritation and bad temper. Whenever we lose our temper and take it out on people around us we do harm, not only to them, but to ourselves. People project their inner problems onto others and fail to see that the cause and remedy lie within. I once witnessed a Sunday school superintendent lose his temper during a committee meeting. When another committee member confronted him and told him that his bad spirit was not in harmony with Christian practice he replied, 'But I have to lose my temper in order to get anything done around here.' This was an excuse, of course, for the Phillips translation of James 1:20 reads: 'For man's temper is never the means of achieving God's true goodness.' Wrong means inevitably lead to wrong ends.

One commentator says of patience, 'This fourth fruit of the Spirit expresses the attitude to people which never loses patience with them, however unreasonable they may be, and never loses hope for them, however unlovely and unteachable they may be.' Notice the words 'never loses patience with them'. How many of us, I wonder, could do that without supernatural help? Archbishop Trench defined the word 'patience' as 'a long holding out of the mind before it gives room to action or to passion, the self-restraint which does not hastily retaliate a wrong'. Moffatt describes patience as 'the tenacity with which faith holds out'. Good temper must not, however, be confused with apathy. In the days of the Early Church, a group called the Stoics made indifference a virtue. They argued, 'Nothing is worth suffering for, so build a wall around your heart and keep out all sense of feeling.' The early Christians did not share that view, however, for Christians care – and because they cared, they suffered. But through the ministry of the Spirit in their lives they found poise and good temper amidst their sufferings. The more we care, the more sensitive we will be to things that are likely to block our goal of caring, and that is why patience is so necessary.

An interesting moment in the life of Saul is recorded in 1 Samuel 10:27: 'But some troublemakers said, "How can this fellow save us?" They despised him and brought him no gifts. But Saul kept silent.' Had Saul maintained that same spirit, his life might not have ended in such a tragic way. A woman, after giving her life to Christ, found herself being provoked by her family. She said, 'I used to have a violent temper and my family were careful how they talked to me. It was a goal of mine always to have the last word. Following my conversion, my family used to test me by saying all the things they knew used to annoy me. If it had not been for the presence of the Spirit in my life, I know I would not have had the patience to handle their remarks. I still have the last word – but the last word is silence.'

Week 5: Supernatural Kindness and Goodness

Opening Icebreaker

The importance of kindness is seen by the fact that an act of kindness lingers on in the memory. Once I was due to speak but was feeling a little weighed down by personal circumstances. Just before I was about to start, a few ladies handed me a little box in which was a beautiful flower along with a message: 'We love you and are praying for you.' That kindness and the spirit that prompted it stood out like a star on a dark night. I have never forgotten it and never will forget it. It will live on within me until the day I die.

Bible Readings

The readings contain references to the concept of death to self as well as kindness and goodness.

Aim of the Session

Kindness is a means of sharing God's love and grace with others, for, although it is firstly an attitude of the heart, it will inevitably be demonstrated by 'acts of kindness'. Supernatural goodness also is a quality that radiates the presence of God flowing through us to those we meet. Kindness and goodness therefore are indispensable fruits of the Spirit to develop in our lives.

George Müller talked about his 'secret death'. In Galatians 2:20 the apostle Paul also talks about a 'death'. In the main, there are two differing views on this passage. One view is that Paul is referring here to the teaching he expounded in Romans 6, namely that when Christ died at Calvary we all 'died' with Him, but because He came back from the dead we must now apply ourselves to appropriating that resurrection power and allow it to work in us to overcome self and sin. Paul's statement about being 'crucified with Christ', it is claimed, has reference to that. Others take the view that Paul is referring to a specific experience in his life following his conversion when his 'old self' (the carnal nature) 'died' to self-interest. With the 'old self' crucified, the self in which Christ lives rises in its stead. Personally, I see truth in both these views. Sanctification is a process but it can also take place at a particular point in time. Many Christians can testify, as did George Müller, that even though they were applying the sanctifying power of the Holy Spirit in their lives day by day, there came a moment or a period when they experienced a critical putting to death of the ego. Not everyone, it seems, is brought by the Spirit to experience sanctification at a particular time, but it is significant that most of the saints whose lives are marked by a high degree of holiness testify to such an experience.

So often in life our first thought is for ourselves. Generally speaking, we are extremely self-centred – everything has an immediate self-reference. Sadly, one Christian I knew was more upset over his own dead dog than a neighbour's dead child. And so deeply ingrained is our self-preoccupation that we ourselves cannot get rid of it. Yet, thankfully, through the work of the Holy Spirit in their lives, there are multitudes whose first thoughts are not for themselves but for the Lord and for others. A minister I once visited who had been struck down with polio anxiously asked me, 'But who will care for my people?' It was not of himself he was thinking, but of others. This selflessness can be explained in only one way: he had died to himself. The centre of life had shifted from self to Christ and thus the fruit of goodness had ripened in his life in much the same way as fruit appears in an orchard.

Week 6: Reliable Faithfulness

Opening Icebreaker
Some professions and people have a bad name for trustworthiness. Our responsibility is that our behaviour should contribute to giving Christianity a name synonymous with faithfulness and reliability.

Bible Readings
The parable of the sower is really the parable of the soil, for the seed was the same in each case but it was the characteristics of the soil that made all the difference. So it is with us that those who are faithful, hear the Word, retain it and persevere, will produce much fruit. Ananias and Sapphira's error was not in keeping back part of the price of the land, but in (apparently) dishonestly claiming that they gave all they received to the apostles (Acts 5:4).

Aim of the Session
The aim of the session is to impress upon us that faithfulness is not an optional extra but a vital quality that forms part of the root system of a mature and flourishing Christian. Over the years, when I have seen a young man or woman on fire for God, I have often said to myself, 'There goes a young person who will make great strides in the kingdom.' But sadly time and time again I have seen them fail in their faithful fulfilment of small obligations. And then I have said to myself, 'Unless there are great changes, that person will end up like the children of Israel in the wilderness – going around in circles.' As God allows challenges in our life they reveal our trustworthiness. For those who are faithful, more will be given. But for those who are unfaithful, their spiritual development and blessings will be limited and they will fall short of their true potential.

It has been said that the ultimate test of a person's character is: Are there any circumstances in which that person will lie? If so, then that person's character is blemished. A Christian worker known to me puts in many hours of service and is prepared to come to the aid of anyone in need but, sadly, he cannot always be relied upon to speak the truth. That lack of honesty cancels out much of the value of his accomplishments. Governments, organisations, institutions and individuals who practise dishonesty will be broken from within. History has proved that. The Roman Empire was destroyed, not from without, but from within – broken upon the rock of its own corruption. Believe me, no one gets away with anything in God's moral universe. No one.

One Christian writer has listed what he believes to be the eight fiercest tests a believer has to face in this world. First, humiliation – a savage and plausible attack on our reputation. Second, suffering – physical, mental or spiritual. Third, bereavement – especially the death of a loved one whose passing was 'untimely'. Fourth, estrangement or treachery from one's family and friends. Fifth, doubt – deep, dark and awful. Sixth, failure – the breaking up of one's life work. Seventh, dereliction – the sense of being forsaken by God. Eighth, a slow, painful and unillumined death. Not all of us encounter all of these trials, but meeting any one of them can be a strong and severe test. It is easy to be faithful when there are no trials or when problems are minor and short lived. Faithfulness embraces the concept of endurance and perseverance over long periods of painful situations. So how does a Christian triumph in the midst of such fierce testings as those listed above? Any triumph we experience at such times is the triumph of the Holy Spirit. He dwells in us, not just for the pleasure of inhabiting our beings, but to lead us to victory over all our problems.

Week 7: Humility and Self-control

Opening Icebreaker

The quality of true spiritual humility is primarily our understanding of our relationship with God and our reverent submission to His will; not inferiority, a false sense of modesty or self-effacement before people. The truly humble before God would then treat others with respect and consideration because we are all made in His image.

Bible Readings

Paul urges us not to think of ourselves more highly than we ought but, by the same token, we should not think of ourselves more lowly than we ought. We must have a sane and balanced estimate of ourselves – one that is neither too high nor too low because after all we are children of God and joint heirs with Christ (Rom. 8:16–17; Gal. 4:7). Humility is rooted in a correct view of God, but it is also fixed in a correct view of ourselves.

Aim of the Session

Without humility and self-control our spiritual lives will be impoverished and there will be a lack of satisfying intimacy with God. We therefore need to understand the true nature of these spiritual fruits and seek to develop them in our personalities. The original Greek word *prautes* is translated in various ways in different translations of the New Testament. One version uses the word 'tolerance', another 'forbearance' and another 'adaptability'. This Greek word has no exact equivalent in English, and after examining the words used in the different translations, my personal opinion is that the Good News Bible gets closest to the true meaning when it uses the word 'humility'. However, we must be careful not to miss the thought that is contained in some of the other words used by translators including gentleness and meekness. Putting them all together, we have a picture of this fruit of the Spirit as a gentle spirit of lowliness and humility with no arrogance but a joyous desire to serve. William Barclay suggests five key areas of humility: a teachable spirit (James 1:21); gentle correction (Gal. 6:1); patient instruction (2 Tim. 2:25); respectful witness (1 Pet. 3:15) and Christlike service (James 3:13).

Self-control helps the Christian to offer to God an obedient personality which is not cloyed by comfort or sluggish from indulgence but sensitive to guidance and ready for all His perfect will. The mother of John Wesley is reported to have said, 'Whatever increases the strength and authority of your body over your mind, however innocent it may be in itself – that thing is sin to you.' David Hill, a Christian writer, puts it this way: 'There is before each one of us an altar of sacrifice, unseen but real and present; and on this altar we are called to offer ourselves. There is some crucifixion of the flesh, some physical self-sacrifice, the abandonment of some bodily indulgence which the spirit of man knows that he is called to make.'

How delighted the body is with the luxuries of life. It has been said that the luxuries of one generation become the bare necessities of the next. If we are thoroughly honest, most of us will admit that self-control is a fruit we most definitely need. One thing the body clamours for is rest and sleep. People differ in the amount of sleep that they need, but we must watch that we do not spend more time in bed than is good for us. I like *The Message* version of Matthew 26:41, 'Stay alert; be in prayer so you don't wander into temptation without even knowing you're in danger. There is a part of you that is eager, ready for anything in God. But there's another part that's as lazy as an old dog sleeping by the fire.'

Notes...

Notes...

Notes...

Latest Resources

The Popular *Cover to Cover* Bible Study Series

1 Corinthians
Growing a Spirit-filled church
ISBN: 978-1-85345-374-8

2 Corinthians
Restoring harmony
ISBN: 978-1-85345-551-3

1,2,3 John
Walking in the truth
ISBN: 978-1-78259-763-6

1 Peter
Good reasons for hope
ISBN: 978-1-78259-088-0

2 Peter
Living in the light of God's promises
ISBN: 978-1-78259-403-1

23rd Psalm
The Lord is my shepherd
ISBN: 978-1-85345-449-3

1 Timothy
*Healthy churches –
effective Christians*
ISBN: 978-1-85345-291-8

2 Timothy and Titus
Vital Christianity
ISBN: 978-1-85345-338-0

Abraham
Adventures of faith
ISBN: 978-1-78259-089-7

Acts 1–12
Church on the move
ISBN: 978-1-85345-574-2

Acts 13–28
To the ends of the earth
ISBN: 978-1-85345-592-6

Barnabas
Son of encouragement
ISBN: 978-1-85345-911-5

Bible Genres
Hearing what the Bible really says
ISBN: 978-1-85345-987-0

Daniel
Living boldly for God
ISBN: 978-1-85345-986-3

David
A man after God's own heart
ISBN: 978-1-78259-444-4

Ecclesiastes
*Hard questions and
spiritual answers*
ISBN: 978-1-85345-371-7

Elijah
A man and his God
ISBN: 978-1-85345-575-9

Elisha
A lesson in faithfulness
ISBN: 978-1-78259-494-9

Ephesians
Claiming your inheritance
ISBN: 978-1-85345-229-1

Esther
For such a time as this
ISBN: 978-1-85345-511-7

Ezekiel
A prophet for all times
ISBN: 978-1-78259-836-7

Fruit of the Spirit
Growing more like Jesus
ISBN: 978-1-85345-375-5

Galatians
Freedom in Christ
ISBN: 978-1-85345-648-0

God's Rescue Plan
*Finding God's fingerprints
on human history*
ISBN: 978-1-85345-294-9

Great Prayers of the Bible
Applying them to our lives today
ISBN: 978-1-85345-253-6

Habakkuk
Choosing God's way
ISBN: 978-1-78259-843-5

Haggai
Motivating God's people
ISBN: 978-1-78259-686-8

Hebrews
Jesus – simply the best
ISBN: 978-1-85345-337-3

Hosea
The love that never fails
ISBN: 978-1-85345-290-1

Isaiah 1–39
Prophet to the nations
ISBN: 978-1-85345-510-0

For current prices or to order, visit **www.cwr.org.uk/shop**
Available online or from Christian bookshops.

Be inspired by God.
Every day.

Confidently face life's challenges by equipping yourself daily with God's Word. There is something for everyone...

Every Day with Jesus
Selwyn Hughes' renowned writing is updated by Mick Brooks for these trusted and popular notes.

Life Every Day
Jeff Lucas helps apply the Bible to daily life through his trademark humour and insight.

Inspiring Women Every Day
Encouragement, uplifting scriptures and insightful daily thoughts for women.

The Manual
Straight-talking guide to help men walk daily with God. Written by Carl Beech, and special guests.

To find out more about all our daily Bible reading notes, or to take out a subscription, visit **www.cwr.org.uk/biblenotes** or call 01252 784700.
Also available in Christian bookshops.

 Printed format **Large print format** **Email format** **Ebook format**

SmallGroup central

All of our small group ideas and resources in one place

Online:

www.smallgroupcentral.org.uk is filled with free video teaching, tools, articles and a whole host of ideas.

On the road:

A range of seminars themed for small groups can be brought to your local community. Contact us at ***hello@smallgroupcentral.org.uk***

In print:

Books, study guides and DVDs covering an extensive list of themes, Bible books and life issues.

Find out more at:
www.smallgroupcentral.org.uk

Courses and events

Waverley Abbey College

Publishing and media

Conference facilities

Transforming lives

CWR's vision is to enable people to experience personal transformation through applying God's Word to their lives and relationships.

Our Bible-based training and resources help people around the world to:
• Grow in their walk with God
• Understand and apply Scripture to their lives
• Resource themselves and their church
• Develop pastoral care and counselling skills
• Train for leadership
• Strengthen relationships, marriage and family life and much more.

Our insightful writers provide daily Bible reading notes and other resources for all ages, and our experienced course designers and presenters have gained an international reputation for excellence and effectiveness.

CWR's Training and Conference Centre in Surrey, England, provides excellent facilities in an idyllic setting – ideal for both learning and spiritual refreshment.

CWR Applying God's Word
to everyday life and relationships

CWR, Waverley Abbey House,
Waverley Lane, Farnham,
Surrey GU9 8EP, UK

Telephone: **+44 (0)1252 784700**
Email: info@cwr.org.uk
Website: www.cwr.org.uk

Registered Charity No. 294387
Company Registration No. 1990308